Little

Scavenger

by Linda Prieto

To: The children of Rowlett, TX

Enjoy !

Linda Foust Prieto

⊕ **Strategic Book Publishing**

Strategic Book Publishing
An imprint of Strategic Book Group
P.O. Box 333
Durham CT 06422
www.StrategicBookGroup.com

ISBN: 978-1-60860-885-0

Printed in the United States of America

Illustrations art, book cover art and book layout by
kalpart team - www.kalpart.com

This book is dedicated to my family, the Foust clan, past, present, and future. Without their closeness, sense of adventure, sense of humor and love for each other, this story would have never been passed on through generations.

Acknowledgements

Credit for the published book goes to the staff of AEG Publishing that helped me through this process. Their support at each step made the final product attainable for a first time author like myself. An extra "Thank You" goes to the illustrators K.J. and team for such a wonderful job of making this story come to life.

SPECIAL THANKS

Special "Thanks" goes to my husband, Raymond Prieto who's vision and support was instrumental in getting this story published.

I hope your families enjoy it as much as ours have through the years!

Synopsis

The events of this story are true. They will take you back to a simpler time.

On many occasions the entire families of Ted, Ed, and Bill Foust would listen as the tales of their father's childhood, spent in Kansas during the depression era, would fill the air.

Unlike in many families, the stories we heard were funny and heartwarming. If you knew the "Foust boys," you would know why! These memories are great things to have, and I want to share one of them with everyone.

Jimmie, the little scavenger, lived a few short years in Galena, Kansas, but in our family he lives on through this story and hopefully for many years to come for other children and their families.

Jimmie was a squirrel that was acquired by the trading of a Daisy rifle. (Don't tell Ma.) You will be going along for a wonderful journey with Jimmie and his new family. In that story Jimmie is their pet and their constant companion. Jimmie was a remarkable pet; he seemed to understand that he was part of their family. To see the boys and their bond with Jimmie grow is something you will enjoy.

Unfortunately, as in many real life memories, there isn't always a happy ending. Jimmie's life is taken in one split second, and the whole town of Galena, Kansas, expresses their love for the "little scavenger."

Contents

Chapter 1

It was a cold and windy day when Ed and Bill Foust set out to the local woods. They wanted to see what they could shoot with their new Daisy air rifle. As they were entering the woods, they came upon a playmate of theirs, Ted Scutter. Ted had something in his hands. The way he was holding it, you would have thought it was a piece of candy or a cookie he had taken while his ma wasn't looking. After some feudin' and fussin', Ed and Bill finally talked Ted into letting them see what he had clutched in his hands.

Ted opened his hands slowly, and the boys saw a little ball of fur.

"It's nothing but an old coon tail," Bill said disappointedly.

"No it ain't," said Ed; "it's moving!"

"Of course," Ted laughed. "It's a little squirrel; ain't you ever seen one afor?"

Sure enough it was a little squirrel. Ted put it down on a bed of leaves where Ed and Bill got a better look at it. It was the cutest little thing. He was just a baby, and his eyes weren't even open. He was a little ball of fur lying there making squeaky noises that made the boys laugh. Ed and Bill had never seen a baby squirrel before, and they decided it would be fun to keep a baby squirrel like this one.

"Hey, Ted, do you want this squirrel?" inquired Ed.

"What ya give me for it? " replied Ted.

"What ya want?" asked Ed.

"How about your new Daisy rifle; I'd sure like to have it."

"Oh, I don't know; I don't think Ma would like it if I gave my new rifle away."

"You're not giving your rifle away; you're atrading it fur a baby squirrel."

"Okay, here's the gun, but don't tell my ma where you got it."

Chapter 2

The boys returned home with their prized possession. When they got home, Ed told his ma he had a baby squirrel.

"Baby squirrel!" his ma exclaimed. "You can't keep it in the house; you'll have to get rid of it."

"But, Ma, he is so cute, and he won't take up much room. Bill and I will take care of him."

"I don't care; I won't have a squirrel sleeping in my house!"

Then Ed brought the squirrel in to show Ma. He was hoping that she would change her mind. The minute Ma saw the squirrel her heart melted like ice. Even Ma couldn't resist his squeaky little noises.

"Well, what are you going to call him?" asked Ma.

Ed replied, "He is mine, and I think he looks like Uncle Jimmie. His hair is all messed up, too. I'm going to call him Jimmie."

So, little Jimmie was now a part of the family. The problem was where Jimmie was going to sleep. He was so tiny he couldn't sleep with the boys because he might be squashed, and if he slept in the open he might freeze to death. Well, good ole Ma came to the rescue. She had the place for the little one. Ma went to the kitchen and brought back a little round one gallon crock just big enough for Jimmie. The boys got some rags and put them in it. They then set it on their dresser. Ed picked up little Jimmie and put him in his new bed.

Now the problem that had to be solved was how they were going to feed this little scavenger. Luckily for Jimmie, Ma was always thinking. She told them to go and borrow a little doll bottle from the neighbor's girl and bring it to the barn. The boys went and got the bottle. When they returned to the barn, they found Ma standing by their pet goat. They were wondering just what she was planning to do. They soon found out. Ma took the bottle and filled it with goat milk. When they fed it to Jimmie, he wrinkled his nose with satisfaction and soon fell fast asleep.

Jimmie was always doing something to make the boys laugh. Every morning while Ma was cooking breakfast, little Jimmie would climb up on her shoulder and sit there. When it was time for the boys to get up and get ready for school, she always sent Jimmie to wake them up. Jimmie would talk to Ma until she said, "Okay, it's time." At that moment

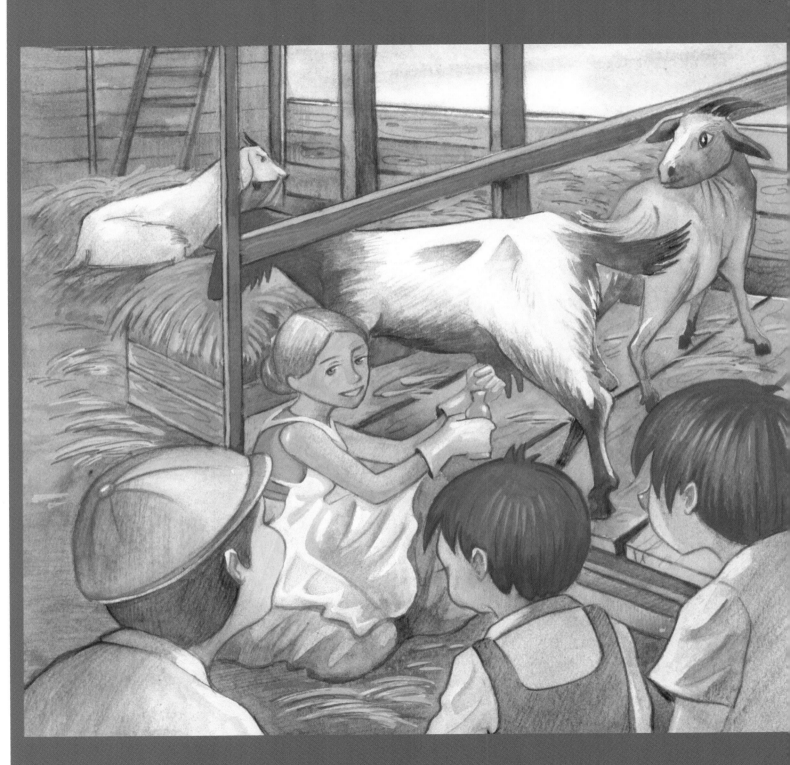

Jimmie would scamper down from Ma's shoulder, and upstairs he went as fast as his little feet could carry him.

First he would jump up on Ed's bed. He would get under the covers and nibble on his toes. Ed, not wanting to get up, would merely move his feet to the other side of the bed and go back to sleep. Jimmie wouldn't give up; he got back on the top of the covers and headed for little Ed's nose. He would slowly sneak up to his chest, and all of a sudden he would pounce onto Ed's face. Jimmie would nibble and scratch his nose until Ed was forced to surrender and get up. After Jimmie got Ed up, he headed for Bill's bed. Jimmie's favorite little trick to get Bill up was chewing on his cold ears that were sticking out of the covers. It took only a couple of little bites before Bill was up and dressing for school.

Jimmie, having done his job for this morning, would scamper downstairs and back to Ma's shoulder again. Every morning she gave Jimmie a reward for getting the boys up. He would sit on her shoulder and make squeaky little noises until Ma reached down into her apron and pulled a walnut out and handed it to him. Jimmie would take the walnut in his hands and then put it into his mouth. This made him look like a little kid with a jaw breaker. Down to the floor he would run. Jimmie had a favorite place where he ate nuts. He would back up into a corner over by the sink and sit up and eat them. When he was finished with the shell, he would neatly add it to his stacked pile and return to his little one-gallon crock for a nap.

Chapter 3

All the kids in the neighborhood loved to play with Jimmie, and Jimmie liked to tease all of them. All, that is, but one. His name was Orval Smart. Orval liked Jimmie, but he tried to play too rough with him. Every time Jimmie would scamper across the room, Orval would slap him back about two feet. Poor little Jimmie didn't have any protection from him. Then one day Jimmie decided he had had enough of Orval Smart. Jimmie saw Orval starting from across the street towards him. He took off like a streak, and into the house he went. Ma had an old clothes hamper in her closet. Jimmie had chewed a hole in the bottom of it and made a nest to hide the nuts. Whenever he wanted to hide from Orval Smart, into the closet he would go and into his little nest. Jimmie would not come out for anyone until Orval had left.

Forty Fleelen owned the local store where Jimmie loved to visit. Every Sunday morning Bill would put on his Sunday go-to-meeting overalls and head for Forty's store to sit around the potbelly stove. Bill wanted to warm his hands and listen to the old men jaw about something that didn't make sense to him. At least it was something to do to get out of going to church. Jimmie always went with Bill. Jimmie didn't want to stay all alone while his playmates went to church. He had his own special compartment where he rode while Bill walked. He would climb up Bill's leg and into his shirt pocket. When they reached the store, he would stick his little paws over Bill's overalls and listen to all the gossip, with Bill.

After a couple of trips to the store, temptation was too great for Jimmie to take any longer. Forty kept the assorted nuts in a big bin in front of the store window. Bill felt Jimmie slowly sneak down his pant leg, and Bill saw him scamper across the floor. I guess you know where he went. That's right, right to the nut bin. He would fill his mouth and hold one nut in his paws; then, he would head back to Bill--up Bill's leg and back into his pocket. Before Bill left the store, his pocket was bulging with little Jimmie's stolen loot. Forty enjoyed seeing Jimmie come into the store. Jimmie would make up to Forty as if he knew Forty was the man that owned the store. Forty got so used to seeing Jimmie come into the store every Sunday morning that he left the candy jars on the counter open so that Jimmie could help himself to a treat of rock candy.

Jimmie went everywhere with the boys. The Christmas before Jimmie was found by the boys, they got a little red wagon. It was always full of fishing poles, as well as everything little boys need to catch the big one that usually gets away. The boys were at the stage where they liked to go and stay overnight away from home. They always took Jimmie with them. Bill would pack the food they needed, and Ed would get their gear ready to go. Off they went. Ed was the eldest, so he pulled the wagon. Bill was supposed to walk behind it, seeing that nothing would fall off before they got there; but Bill was still pretty young, and his feet couldn't carry him very long. When he got tired, he would sit on the edge of the wagon for a while.

Jimmie was a privileged character when they went on their fishing trips; he got to ride on the top of their gear. He thought he was the king sitting on his throne. When he got hungry, he would topple off the gear, run to a tree nearby, and take a nut along with him for a snack. Jimmie never got tired of going fishing. In fact, the boys couldn't sneak away from him even if they wanted to go without him.

When the boys reached the fishing hole, Jimmie would sit by the hole and wait for the boys to start fishing. Jimmie, being a scavenger, couldn't sit still in one place very long. While the boys were busy fishing, Jimmie would take off for the local woods. The boys could hear him in the trees talking to all the other little squirrels. Jimmie would always come back when they called him, no matter what he was doing or where he had wandered. I guess Jimmie found out from the other squirrels what an easy life he really had with the boys.

Back home again, Jimmie would scamper back into the big tree in the front yard. While the boys were at school, Jimmie would sit up in the tree and chatter to all the people that passed under him. Everyone in town knew Jimmie and always stopped to say, "Hi," to him.

Chapter 4

One time the family decided to go on a vacation. Of course, Jimmie was to go too. At that time the boys' parents didn't have much money, but they always saw to it that the boys had a good time. Bright and early the boys helped their ma pack the suitcases into the car. Pa was in the barn making sure everything was okay. It was a pretty spring day; everyone was excited about the trip, even Jimmie. Jimmie also packed some of his things for the trip. Ma put his little one gallon crock into the car. While they weren't looking, Jimmie ran up the tree and brought back three nuts out of his winter supply and put them in his bed. I guess he was afraid there might not be any nuts where they were going.

It was a long and dusty trip to Kansas City, but the boys loved every minute. They didn't get much chance to go for rides. Jimmie didn't like the wind coming through the window, so he slept under the seat most of the way. By that evening the family reached Kansas City. They decided to go straight to the hotel and get some sleep before they looked over the town. Pa signed the family in, and they went up to their room. When Bill got up there, he asked Ed if he had Jimmie. Ed said, "I thought you had him."

In the excitement of seeing the big city, the boys had forgotten about little Jimmie. They went back down to the car to look for him, but he wasn't there. They called him, but he didn't come. Ma told the boys to go back up to their room and that Jimmie would probably be back in the morning. The boys went back up to bed, but they didn't sleep because they were worried about Jimmie.

Meanwhile, Jimmie was roaming around town. He had never been that far away from home, and it was exciting to him. He liked to watch all the people. It was Saturday night, and there was a dance in the central park. Jimmie went there for awhile and listened to music. He soon found he was getting tired. He began to wonder if he could find his way back to his family. He wandered around for about an hour. Suddenly it began to rain. It was one of those spring showers. Jimmie didn't give up' he kept on looking.

He finally came to the hotel. He remembered watching the boys climb up the stairs to their room. Now the problem was how he was going to get up there. Then he saw a big tree growing by the side of the hotel. This gave Jimmie an idea. He climbed up the tree and peeked into the dark room. He was all wet now and very sleepy. He sat on the windowsill and chattered and squeaked, hoping one of the boys would hear him. The boys weren't asleep because they were worrying about him. Eventually, Ed got out of bed and brought little Jimmie into the room. He was all wet and looked like a drowned rat. Ed dried him off and put him into his one gallon crock. Jimmie was home again with his family.

Chapter 5

One day, when all the neighborhood kids were outside playing games with Jimmie, a boy came by and asked if he could play too. His name was Paul Ferguson. He weighed about two hundred pounds, but the boys liked him. They let him play. While Paul was hiding, he saw Jimmie take off towards the woods. He thought Jimmie was running away. Paul ran after Jimmie. Before the boys could stop him, Paul was gone. He chased and chased Jimmie. Jimmie thought Paul was playing with him so all of a sudden Jimmie stopped right in front of Paul. Paul was so big and clumsy that he tripped and fell right on Jimmie. Jimmie was dead. The boy's baby, Jimmie, was dead.

Everyone in town was sad when they found out that Jimmie had died. Paul felt worse than anyone; he hadn't meant to hurt Jimmie. By this time Jimmie had become a part of everyone's heart. The family felt they had to do something special for Jimmie before they put him to rest. Ma spent the last of her egg money and bought a piece of black silk to put on the inside of Jimmie's final resting place. It was decided that Jimmie should be buried in his little one gallon crock that belonged to him from the very first day he came into their home. Some of the people in the town came to little Jimmie's funeral.

The place that Jimmie was to be put to rest was his favorite tree in the front yard. People who had seen Jimmie through the years brought him gifts to be buried with him. Forty Freelen, the storeowner, brought a bag of Jimmie's favorite nuts. As Jimmie was being buried, tears came to many people's eyes, and you knew they must have been thinking of the many times they themselves had stopped to talk to Jimmie and Jimmie had talked to them. To this day, every family that has lived in Ted, Bill and Ed's childhood home have been told this story of Jimmie. They are shown his final resting place, below his favorite tree marked with the words **"Jimmie, our beloved little scavenger."**